Wright Brothers

A Buddy Book
by
Sarah Tieck

ABDO
Publishing Company

VISIT US AT

www.abdopublishing.com

Published by ABDO Publishing Company, 4940 Viking Drive, Suite 622, Edina, Minnesota
55435. Copyright © 2007 by Abdo Consulting Group, Inc. International copyrights reserved
in all countries. No part of this book may be reproduced in any form without written
permission from the publisher.

Printed in the United States.

Contributing Editor: Michael P. Goecke
Graphic Design: Jane Halbert
Cover Photograph: Library of Congress
Interior Photographs/Illustrations: Getty Images, Library of Congress, North Wind

Library of Congress Cataloging-in-Publication Data

Tieck, Sarah, 1976–
    The Wright brothers / Sarah Tieck.
       p. cm. — (First biographies. Set V)
    Includes index.
          ISBN 10 1-59679-790-8
          ISBN 13 978-1-59679-790-1
    1. Wright, Wilbur, 1867–1912—Juvenile literature. 2. Wright, Orville, 1871–1948—
Juvenile literature. 3. Aeronautics—United States—Biography—Juvenile literature. 4.
Aeronautics—United States—History—Juvenile literature. I. Title II. Series: Tieck, Sarah,
1976– . First biographies. Set V.

TL540.W7T54 2006
629.130092'2—dc22

                                                                    2005031973

Table Of Contents

Who Are The Wright Brothers?

Wilbur and Orville Wright are famous brothers and aviators.

Wilbur (left) and Orville (right) Wright

Orville and Wilbur Wright are known for their inventions. The brothers lived in the United States at a time when there were no airplanes. Some people were just starting to get cars.

The Wright brothers invented one of the first airplanes that actually flew. One important part of their plane was that it could be controlled. This made it safer for the aviator.

Orville was at the plane's controls for the first flight.

In 1903, Wilbur and Orville's flying machine soared through the air near Kitty Hawk, North Carolina. Some say this was the first flight.

Wilbur and Orville's plane was an important invention. It changed the way people travel. Now, people fly all over the world in airplanes.

The Wright Family

Wilbur Wright was born in New Castle, Indiana, on April 16, 1867. His younger brother, Orville Wright, was born in Dayton, Ohio, on August 19, 1871.

Wilbur (left) and Orville (right) as children.

Orville and Wilbur's mother was Susan Wright. Their father was Bishop Milton Wright. Orville and Wilbur had five other brothers and sisters. There was Reuchlin, Lorin, Otis, Ida, and Katharine. Otis and Ida were twins. They died when they were still babies.

Orville and Wilbur's mother took care of the family. Their father was a bishop in the United Brethren Church. Because of this, the Wright family moved many times.

Bishop Milton Wright

Growing Up

There are many stories about Orville and Wilbur when they were children. They both loved to learn. Luckily, there was a big library in their home.

Orville and Wilbur were part of a creative family. When their father traveled for work, he brought home presents. He told his children stories about what he'd seen. They wanted to see the world, too.

The Wright family lived in this house in Dayton, Ohio.

Orville works in the bike shop with Edwin H. Sines, a neighbor and friend.

Orville and Wilbur loved learning about mechanics. They were also interested in business. They would make toys and sell them. Orville loved bicycles. So, he and Wilbur started to rent and sell bicycles.

Orville and Wilbur printed a weekly newspaper, too. It was called the *West Side News*. Sometimes, Katharine and other family members helped.

Learning To Fly

Some say Orville and Wilbur first got interested in flying machines as children. There is a story that their father bought them a toy helicopter. It is said that Orville and Wilbur loved the toy and played with it for hours.

Otto Lilienthal's glider

A famous aviator named Otto Lilienthal died in 1896. Orville and Wilbur were interested in what he had learned and invented. Around 1899, the brothers began to teach themselves about aeronautics.

Many other people tried to invent flying machines. Most of these didn't fly. Orville and Wilbur started to invent flying machines and gliders. These didn't fly, either. The brothers wanted to figure out why the machines wouldn't fly.

A view of Wilbur gliding.

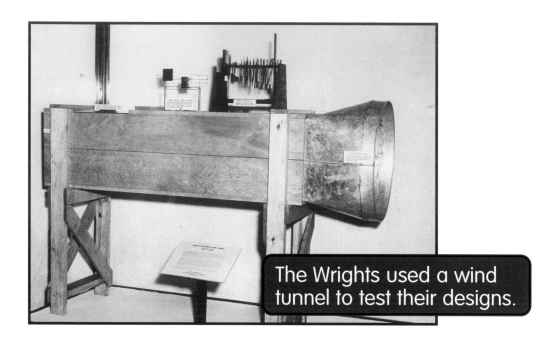

The Wrights used a wind tunnel to test their designs.

As they did research, Orville and Wilbur got an idea. They realized that the plane needed to be controlled. They built a glider with special instruments. These instruments helped control the plane and make it easier to fly. With the instruments, the plane could turn and go up and down.

This new glider flew, but only for a short time. Orville and Wilbur wanted to make a flying machine that would stay in the air. So, they decided to make a plane with a gasoline engine. This took a long time. The engine needed to be light so the plane could take off and fly. After many hours and days of working, the Wright brothers made their first powered aircraft.

This is part of a 1903 motor that the Wrights built.

The First Flight

Orville and Wilbur Wright flew their airplane for the first time near Kitty Hawk, North Carolina. This happened on December 17, 1903.

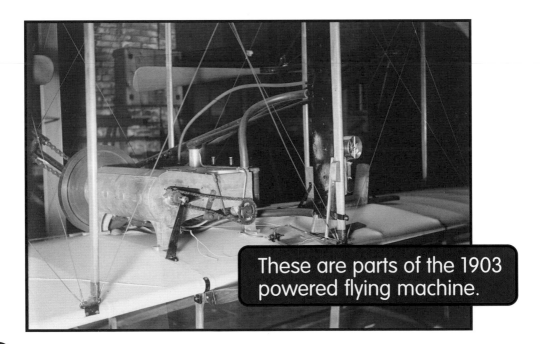

These are parts of the 1903 powered flying machine.

The first flight happened around 10:35 AM.

Orville was the first to fly the airplane. That first flight was only about 12 seconds long. The brothers flew three more times that day. Wilbur is known for the longest flight. He flew 852 feet (260 m) in about one minute.

December 17, 1903, is a very famous day. The Wright brothers proved they had made a flying machine that could actually fly! More important, it was safer because it could be controlled.

After the first flight, Orville and Wilbur knew they had more work to do. They wanted to make their plane better. So, they kept making changes and flew many more times. As they learned new things and got more ideas, they made new airplanes.

Many stories were written about the Wright brothers.

THE DAYTON DAILY NEWS.

WRIGHT'S OFFICIAL FLIGHT A SUCCESS; FULFILLS GOVERNMENT REQUIREMENTS

The Washington Times

Breaking World's Aeroplane Record

WRIGHT'S AEROPLANE, IN THE AIR 57 MINUTES, MAKES WORLD RECORD

MR. ORVILLE WRIGHT SECURES THE ALTITUDE FLYING RECORD

PRESIDENT TAFT PRESENTS MEDALS TO WRIGHT BROTHERS AT WHITE HOUSE IN HONOR OF THEIR AERIAL TRIUMPHS

A Changing World

For a while, no one knew what the Wright brothers had invented. Then, Orville and Wilbur decided to sell their airplanes. In 1905, they contacted the U.S. government and many businesses.

However, many of these places refused. Airplanes were brand-new at this time. Many people didn't believe it was possible to fly. Others wanted to try to build their own plane.

Wilbur often taught others to fly. This flight happened in France in 1908.

In time, people's opinions toward flight changed. Around 1910, people began to get very interested in airplanes and flying. The Wright brothers became known all over the world for their planes. They did flying shows.

Then, they opened the Wright Company in New York City. This was a business that made airplanes. People began to order airplanes. As more people got interested in airplanes, Orville and Wilbur taught others to fly them.

Hard Times

The Wright brothers began to have problems. A man named Samuel P. Langley said he invented the first airplane. Also, a plane that Orville was flying crashed during an important test. His passenger died, and the plane needed to be fixed and changed.

These problems made Orville and Wilbur worried and sad. In 1912, Wilbur got very sick. He died of typhoid fever on May 30, 1912.

Orville was very sad to lose Wilbur. In 1915, he sold the Wright Company. He wanted to do more of the inventing work he'd done with Wilbur. This was the work he loved, and he was good at it.

Orville opened the Wright Aeronautical Laboratory. There, he made many inventions. He kept working to improve airplanes for the rest of his life.

Orville Wright (left) received the Daniel Guggenheim Medal from W.F. Durand.

Orville won awards for his work at the Wright Aeronautical Laboratory. Orville died on January 30, 1948.

An Important Invention

Many people say the Wright brothers changed the way people travel. They have been honored for their work in many ways.

Today, Wright Brothers National Memorial is located at Kitty Hawk.

Both Orville and Wilbur were added to the Hall of Fame for Great Americans in New York City.

Also, there is a monument at Kitty Hawk for them. It is called the Wright Brothers National Memorial. There is a museum. And, visitors can climb to the top of Kill Devil Hill to see where the airplanes took off.

Orville and Wilbur's airplane is at the National Air and Space Museum in Washington, D.C.

Today, people can fly all over the world because of Orville and Wilbur Wright.

Important Dates

April 16, 1867 Wilbur Wright is born.

August 19, 1871 Orville Wright is born.

December 17, 1903 Orville and Wilbur's airplane flies for the first time at Kitty Hawk, North Carolina.

1909 Orville and Wilbur create the Wright Company. It is located in New York City. It manufactures airplanes.

1910-1912 Orville and Wilbur teach other people how to fly airplanes.

May 30, 1912 Wilbur dies of typhoid fever.

1913 Orville wins an award for his inventions.

1915 Orville retires from the Wright Company.

1929 Orville is awarded the first Daniel Guggenheim Medal. It honors the work that he and Wilbur did to create airplanes.

January 30, 1948 Orville dies.

Important Words

aeronautical laboratory a room or building where people work on making aircraft.

aeronautics the science of making and flying aircraft.

aviator a pilot, or a person who flies airplanes.

bishop a high-ranking minister who is the head of a church district.

control to guide the movements of a machine.

flying machine airplane.

glider an aircraft that doesn't have an engine, but flies using air currents.

mechanics how machines work.

Web Sites

To learn more about the Wright Brothers, visit ABDO Publishing Company on the World Wide Web. Web site links about the Wright Brothers are featured on our Book Links page. These links are routinely monitored and updated to provide the most current information available.

www.abdopublishing.com

Index